EARTH SCIENCE PROJECTS
for kids

A PROJECT GUIDE TO

EARTHQUAKES

Claire O'Neal

Mitchell Lane
PUBLISHERS

P.O. Box 196
Hockessin, Delaware 19707
Visit us on the web: www.mitchelllane.com
Comments? email us: mitchelllane@mitchelllane.com

A Project Guide to:
Earthquakes • Earth's Waters •
Rocks and Minerals • The Solar System • Volcanoes •
Wind, Weather, and The Atmosphere

PUBLISHER'S NOTE: The facts on which the story in this book is based have been thoroughly researched. Documentation of such research can be found on page 44. While every possible effort has been made to ensure accuracy, the publisher will not assume liability for damages caused by inaccuracies in the data, and makes no warranty on the accuracy of the information contained herein. The Internet sites referenced herein were active as of the publication date. Due to the fleeting nature of some web sites, we cannot guarantee they will all be active when you are reading this book.

To reflect current usage, we have chosen to use the secular era designations BCE ("before the common era") and CE ("of the common era") instead of the traditional designations BC ("before Christ") and AD (anno Domini, "in the year of the Lord").

The author gratefully acknowledges discussions with Dr. Michael O'Neal.

Library of Congress
Cataloging-in-Publication Data

O'Neal, Claire.
 A project guide to earthquakes / by Claire O'Neal.
    p. cm. — (Earth science projects for kids)
  Includes bibliographical references and index.
  ISBN 978-1-58415-870-7 (lib. bd.)
 1. Earthquakes—Experiments—Juvenile literature. 2. Science projects—Juvenile literature. I. Title.
 QE521.3.O54 2011
 551.22078—dc22
                                               2010030945

Printing   1   2   3   4   5   6   7   8   9

                                               PLB

CONTENTS

EARTHQUAKE!

Imagine a perfectly normal morning in class, the teacher up front, you at your desk. Suddenly, you hear a low rumbling sound and you feel the earth vibrate beneath your feet. Your teacher stops talking in midsentence, looking out the window. You follow his gaze, expecting to see a bulldozer rolling by. Instead you see the trees flopping wildly back and forth, though you know it's not a windy day. "Everyone under your desk!" the teacher yells, and you don't hesitate. You know now that you're in the middle of an earthquake. Although the intense shaking lasts for only a few seconds, the excitement makes this unusual event seem to last much longer.

Today, somewhere on Earth, an earthquake will happen. In fact, according to the U.S. Geological Survey (USGS), 500,000 detectable earthquakes occur each year. Millions more are too small to be felt. Some are strong enough to make the ground vibrate, rattling dishes in cabinets and damaging stiff structures such as brick chimneys. A few very strong earthquakes cause landslides, tsunamis, or even change the course of rivers. Strong quakes near cities can turn skyscrapers into rubble, push houses down cliffs, or rip streets apart. Every year, thousands of people worldwide lose their homes—and some their lives—in earthquakes.

To us, Earth's surface seems quiet, still, and unchanging. In fact, the surface is slowly and constantly moving. Earth's rocky outer surface—known as the **lithosphere**—is made up of large pieces called plates.

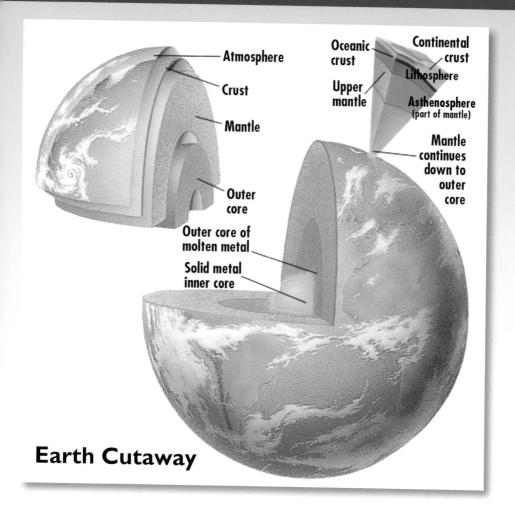

Atmosphere

Crust

Mantle

Oceanic crust

Continental crust

Lithosphere

Upper mantle

Asthenosphere
(part of mantle)

Mantle continues down to outer core

Outer core

Outer core of molten metal

Solid metal inner core

Earth Cutaway

Some geologists count thirteen major plates, though the exact number is subject to debate. These plates, which are up to 42 miles (68 kilometers) thick, float around on a layer of hot, semi-molten rock called the **asthenosphere**. We feel plate movements as earthquakes.

Seismologists study how, when, and where earthquakes happen in order to understand more about our planet and prepare communities for earth-shaking disasters. You can explore what we know about earthquakes through the simple experiments and projects you'll find in this book. Whether for a school project or just for fun, you'll learn to think like a scientist and satisfy your curiosity about earthquakes, all while using materials you probably already have at home.

EGG EARTH

If you could travel straight down to the center of the earth, you would see that our planet is made of layers. We live on the thinnest layer, the lithosphere, which is 4 to 5 miles (6 to 7 kilometers) thick under oceans, but 20 to 25 miles (35 to 40 kilometers) thick under continents. The lithosphere floats atop the asthenosphere, the topmost layer of the **mantle**. The mantle is 1,900 miles (3,000 kilometers) thick, made of rock so hot that it slowly flows. The liquid outer core lies below the mantle and is 1,400 miles (2,250 kilometers) thick. This layer contains pure heavy metals such as nickel and iron. The inner core lies at the center of the planet, a solid ball of iron and nickel 1,540 miles (2,500 kilometers) in diameter. At 4300°C (2400°F), the hot inner core is kept solid only by the pressure of the weight of the layers above it.

You can make a model of Earth's layers with a soft-boiled egg.

Materials
- **an adult**
- pot
- stove
- water
- egg
- tongs or spoon
- timer
- plate
- sharp knife

Instructions

1. Under **adult supervision**, fill a pot with enough water to cover an egg. Remove the egg and bring the pot to a rolling boil. Using tongs or a spoon, gently place the egg into the boiling water. Return the water to a rolling boil; once it reaches that point, set your timer for exactly 3 minutes. When time is up, rinse the egg immediately under cold water until it is warm to the touch.

2. Crack the shell by rolling the egg under your hand on a hard surface. Imagine that the egg is the Earth. These shell pieces act like the Earth's plates. Gently squeeze the egg until the shell pieces move. Some pieces move away from each other, exposing the white "mantle" beneath. Other pieces of shell move toward each other, either colliding or one diving under another. Some pieces of shell will slide past another. These all represent different kinds of plate movements, which will be studied in detail in the next experiment.

3. Put the egg on a plate. Have **an adult** use a sharp knife to cut the egg in half, shell and all. The egg in cross-section represents the earth's layers—the slightly runny yolk symbolizes the outer core, the white is the mantle, and the thin shell is the lithosphere. If you boiled your egg a little longer, you would have a hard yolk, like the solid inner core.

GRAHAM CRACKER FAULTS

Eggshells illustrate the idea of plates, but their small size makes it difficult to really see what's happening where the plates meet. These places are called **faults**, and they are where earthquakes occur. Four different types of faults are possible, depending on the direction the plates are moving and how heavy they are relative to each other.

1) **Transform fault**: The edges of the plates slide against each other. A famous example is the San Andreas Fault in California.

2) **Subduction zone**: As two plates push against each other, the denser plate slips below the lighter one. A subduction zone can create a deep trench where the lower plate slides into the mantle. Many volcanoes are found above subduction zones. The subduction zone where the Pacific Plate slides under the North American Plate creates the volcanoes of the U.S. Pacific Northwest, for example. Magma created from the melting lower plate rises up through cracks in the upper plate. There are many subduction zones underwater. Earthquakes there can cause dangerous tsunamis.

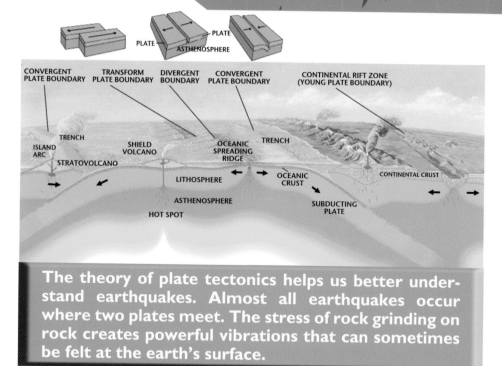

CONVERGENT PLATE BOUNDARY · TRANSFORM PLATE BOUNDARY · DIVERGENT BOUNDARY · CONVERGENT PLATE BOUNDARY · CONTINENTAL RIFT ZONE (YOUNG PLATE BOUNDARY)

PLATE · PLATE · ASTHENOSPHERE

TRENCH · ISLAND ARC · STRATOVOLCANO · SHIELD VOLCANO · OCEANIC SPREADING RIDGE · TRENCH · LITHOSPHERE · OCEANIC CRUST · CONTINENTAL CRUST · ASTHENOSPHERE · HOT SPOT · SUBDUCTING PLATE

The theory of plate tectonics helps us better understand earthquakes. Almost all earthquakes occur where two plates meet. The stress of rock grinding on rock creates powerful vibrations that can sometimes be felt at the earth's surface.

3) **Continental collision**: Plates push against each other and crumple. The Himalayas were created this way about 40 to 50 million years ago, when the Indian Plate slammed into the Eurasian Plate. The material of both continental plates buckled and was pushed upward, creating the most spectacular mountains on Earth.

4) **Divergent boundary**: Plates pull away from each other. Examples of this movement include the Mid-Atlantic Ridge and the African Rift Zone.

Mid-Atlantic Ridge in Iceland

Take a closer look at these cracks in the earth, using graham crackers and frosting to make a delicious model of plate movement atop the mantle. Brittle graham crackers model the earth's plates quite well. For best results, use fresh ones at each step.

Materials
- waxed paper
- frosting or peanut butter
- table knife or spoon
- graham crackers

Divergent boundary

Instructions

1. Lay a sheet of waxed paper on a flat surface. Spread a thick layer of frosting in the middle.

2. Lay two graham crackers next to each other, flat on top of the frosting. Gently press down on the graham cracker "crust" to stick the plates into the frosting "mantle."

3. Gently push the crackers apart from each other, forming a divergent boundary. A rift forms between the plates, where frosting magma oozes up.

Subduction zone

4. Push the crackers toward each other. As they approach, pick up the edge of one so that the other can slide underneath, creating a subduction zone. Keep sliding the crackers against each other. Is their motion smooth or rough?

5. Wet the edge of one cracker and again push them together. This time, let the crackers collide and crumple to create a collision zone. The graham cracker crust piles up to create a "mountain range."

6. Last, create a transform fault. Touch two fresh crackers together and try to slide them past each other. Their rough, brittle edges will catch against each other; movement comes only when crumbs break free. These sudden move-ments mimic those of the San Andreas Fault in California.

Collision zone

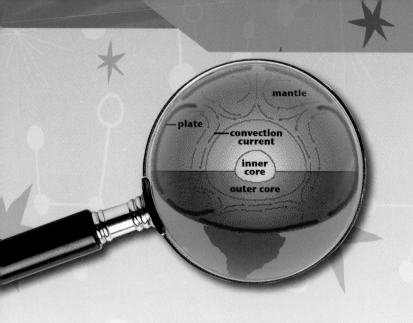

mantle

plate

convection
current

inner
core

outer core

STOVETOP
CONVECTION

In the previous experiment, your fingers provided plate-moving power from above. In reality, the earth's plates move because of **convection** from within the earth. The inner core heats the outer core and mantle. Heated mantle rock becomes less dense and rises toward the earth's surface. As it rises, it moves away from the heat source. Slowly it cools, becoming denser, and sinks back toward the core. This motion, called convection, describes how material in the mantle constantly moves in giant circles. The paths the liquid follows are called convection currents.

Convection currents in the asthenosphere are near the earth's surface, forcing the earth's plates to move. This movement is extremely slow. Many plates move 1.4 inches (3.5 centimeters) per year—as fast as your fingernails grow—but the force is strong enough to literally move mountains!

Convection currents occur in an identical way on the stovetop in your kitchen, where a burner performs the same role as the earth's core. You can observe convection currents in action with the following project.

Materials

- **an adult**
- stove
- pot
- water
- rice
- toast, cut into 1-inch squares
- tongs
- oven mitt

Instructions

1. With the help of **an adult**, bring a pot ²/₃ full of water to a rolling boil. Throw in a few grains of rice and watch the paths they take through the liquid. The rice follows a circular pattern through the water as the grains fall to the bottom and then are buoyed up again by the motion of the heated water.

2. The circular convection motion throughout the liquid creates currents on the surface that can carry floating objects, such as toast "continents." Wearing an oven mitt and using tongs, gently place toast pieces flat on the surface of the boiling water. Watch as the pieces move around on the currents. They move slowly toward and away from each other, some crashing together, some diving underneath others—just like earth's plates do.

PLATE TECTONICS: CONTINENTS IN MOTION

Tiny pieces of toast that are jostled by convection are one thing, but is it really possible to move whole continents that way? Scientists in 1912 didn't think so. That's when German scientist Alfred Wegener identified the same plant fossils in both South America and Africa, dating from 300 million years ago. He found other fossil matches between North America and Europe, and also between Madagascar and India. Though these places are literally oceans apart on today's map, Wegener noticed that their coastlines fit together like pieces of a puzzle. He suggested that all the continents were joined 200 million years ago in an enormous supercontinent he called Pangaea ("All Lands").

Scientists thought Wegener was crazy until 1962, when Harry Hess discovered seafloor spreading. Over time, Hess said, the divergent boundary of the Mid-Atlantic Ridge is slowly pushing the continental plates in opposite directions. South America and Africa are still moving away from each other. This movement is called **plate tectonics**.

See if you can piece together the Pangaea puzzle, just like Wegener did.

Active Volcanoes, Plate Tectonics, and the "Ring of Fire"

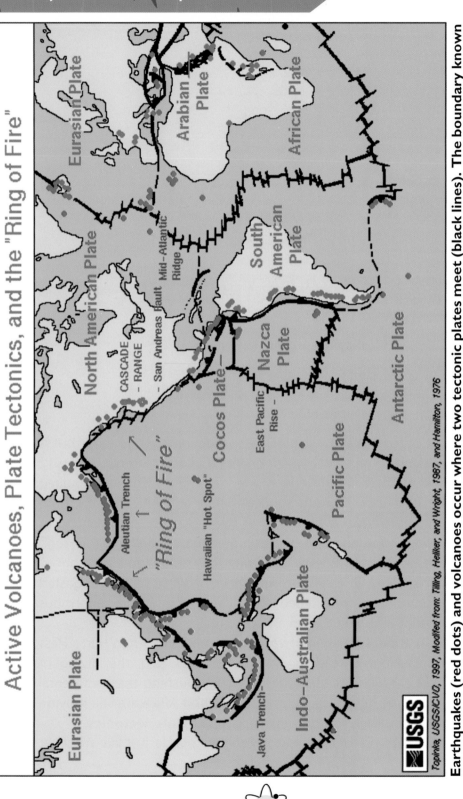

Eurasian Plate

Arabian Plate

African Plate

North American Plate

Mid-Atlantic Ridge

San Andreas Fault

CASCADE - RANGE

South American Plate

Nazca Plate

Antarctic Plate

"Ring of Fire"

Aleutian Trench

Hawaiian "Hot Spot"

Cocos Plate—

East Pacific Rise –

Pacific Plate

Indo–Australian Plate

Java Trench–

Eurasian Plate

Topinka, USGS/CVO, 1997, Modified from: Tilling, Heliker, and Wright, 1987, and Hamilton, 1976

Earthquakes (red dots) and volcanoes occur where two tectonic plates meet (black lines). The boundary known as the Ring of Fire—where the heavy Pacific Plate plunges under its lighter continental neighbors—brings massive earthquakes and explosive volcanic eruptions to heavily populated areas around the Pacific Rim.

250 Million years ago

200 Million years ago

150 Million years ago

100 Million years ago

50 Million years ago

Current

Materials

- large map of the world (If you have access to the Internet, you can print one)
- scissors
- card stock
- glue

15

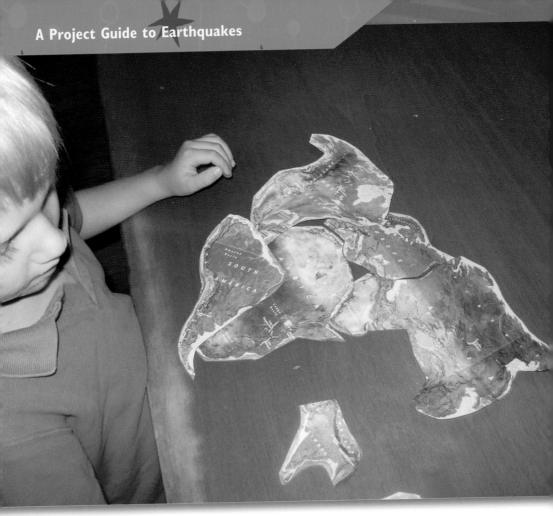

Instructions

1. Cut the continents out of the world map along their boundaries. Glue them onto card stock to make them sturdier.

2. As late as 200 million years ago, all the continents were part of a single supercontinent called Pangaea. Can you put this world back together again?

3. Keep in mind that plate boundaries can change over time. What kinds of motions did the continents have to do to break away from this shape? Are they still making those motions today?

4. Use the Internet to find a map that shows the directions in which the plates are currently moving. Draw arrows on your continents to reflect this motion. Which boundaries are convergent, divergent, or transform? What do you think the earth's continents will look like in the future?

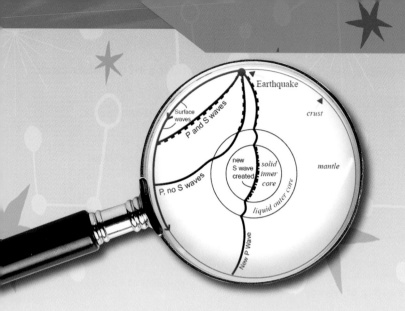

Earthquake

crust

Surface
waves

P and S waves

new
S wave
created

solid
inner
core

mantle

P, no S waves

liquid outer core

New P Wave

ELASTIC EARTHQUAKES

Just like graham crackers, real crustal plates are rough and surprisingly
strong. Convection forces the plates together along fault lines, but
when jagged edges of plates get stuck together, the force can build up
for years. Rocks along the fault bend and break from the pressure.
Thus, sometimes plates move only when the pull from convection
becomes strong enough to break whatever was holding them in place.
Movement along faults can be sudden, releasing energy in the form of
an earthquake.

This idea of plate movement is called **elastic rebound** —"elastic"
because the plates bend under the strain, "rebound" because they snap
out of that bend once they move. Use your knuckles to visualize elastic
rebound: Ball your hands into fists and nest your knuckles against each
other. Pressing your fists together, try to slide your knuckles across each
other in opposite directions. At first your hands move slightly, and you
can feel your skin pulling. When you apply enough force, your knuckles
slide past each other in a sudden, quick movement.

You can demonstrate elastic rebound in a scientific way by dragging
bricks on a rough surface, such as a sidewalk. The texture of the brick
against concrete mimics a rough plate junction. A bungee cord stores

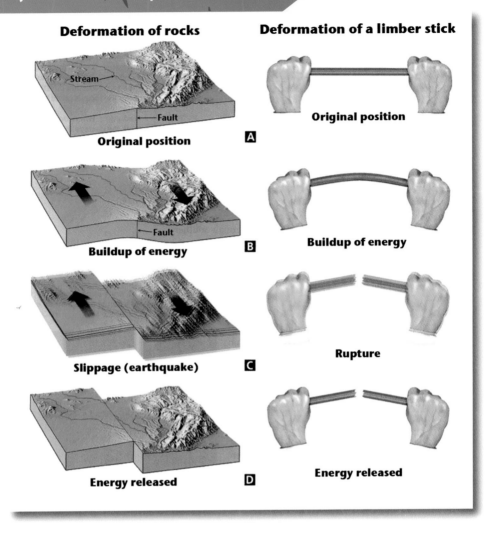

Deformation of rocks

Stream

Fault

Original position

A

Buildup of energy

Fault

B

Slippage (earthquake)

C

Energy released

D

Deformation of a limber stick

Original position

Buildup of energy

Rupture

Energy released

your pulling energy, which is released only when the pull becomes greater than the friction holding the brick in place on the sidewalk.

Materials
- 2 bricks
- thick yarn
- scissors
- 6 feet of bungee cord
- 4 feet of nylon rope
- sidewalk chalk
- baby powder
- short bungee cord
- a friend
- board
- grassy area

After you try pulling one brick, try pulling one that trails another.

Instructions

1. Tie a belt of thick yarn around one brick. Connect the bungee cord to one end of the belt. Tie a nylon rope to the free end of the bungee. This gives you a two-stage rope, where the rope closer to the brick is stretchy, but the rope you will pull on is not.

2. Place the brick with its largest face against the sidewalk. Pull it across the sidewalk using your two-stage rope. Have a friend watch carefully, marking the sidewalk at any place where the brick stops moving as you pull it. When it jerks forward, this simulates the jerking, irregular motion of plates that causes earthquakes.

3. Repeat step 2, but first dust the sidewalk with baby powder. How does the brick move now?

4. Place the second brick atop the first. Repeat steps 2 and 3 with this heavier weight to generate more powerful earthquakes.

5. Now place the second brick behind the first, trailing by a short length of bungee cord. Repeat step 2. Notice how one "earthquake" transfers stress to the second brick and causes it to have an earthquake of its own. This represents an aftershock—how a sudden movement along one part of a fault in Earth's crust may trigger movement at another part of the fault.

6. Try pulling your bricks over other surfaces (such as a board or grass) to see how the elastic rebound effect differs on different materials.

SEISMIC SLINKY

Earthquakes occur where tectonic plates meet. Since these boundaries extend all the way through the lithosphere, the **focus**—or point at which the fault first slips—of an earthquake is usually located miles below earth's surface. The point directly above the focus on the surface is the **epicenter**. Energy released at the focus moves outward in waves, traveling through solid rock. When these waves reach the surface, we feel an earthquake.

Earthquakes move through the earth as P-waves and S-waves. P-waves are compression waves. They travel by squeezing and releasing solid or liquid rock, the way sound waves travel through air. P-waves are the fastest type of seismic wave, traveling at up to 8.7 miles (14 kilometers) per second. S-waves are shear waves, or tearing waves. They move in side-to-side patterns through solids, but cannot travel through fluids. S-waves travel at about half the speed of P-waves. When P- and S-waves interact just below the earth's surface, they create a third type of wave called surface waves. These waves cause powerful rolling motions in rock. Though surface waves do not travel far, they cause the most damage to buildings.

You can use a Slinky spring to demonstrate how P- and S-waves travel, because a Slinky's coils act like earth materials. Both are part of a

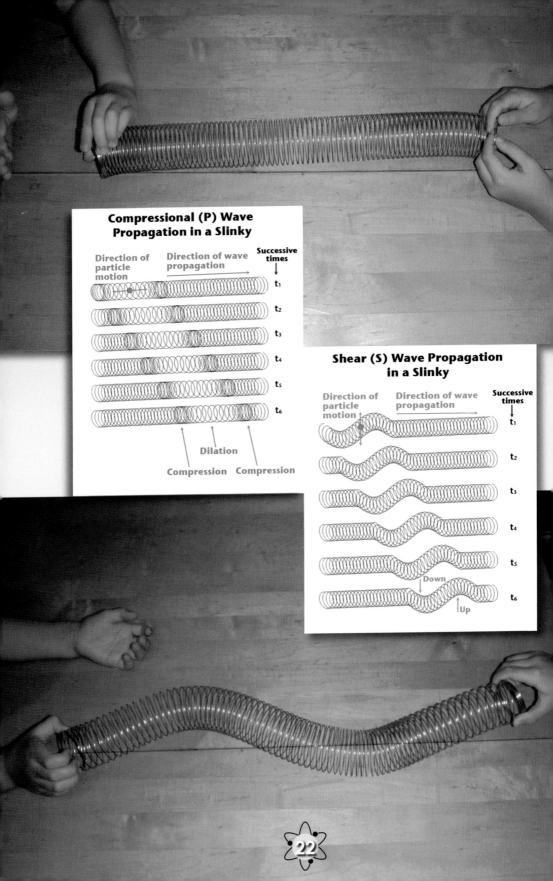

Compressional (P) Wave Propagation in a Slinky

Direction of particle motion

Direction of wave propagation →

Successive times ↓

t₁
t₂
t₃
t₄
t₅
t₆

Dilation

Compression   Compression

Shear (S) Wave Propagation in a Slinky

Direction of particle motion

Direction of wave propagation →

Successive times ↓

t₁
t₂
t₃
t₄
t₅
t₆

Down

Up

larger, connected system (coils are connected to coils and rocks to rocks); and both are stiff yet elastic, bending under force.

Materials
- a friend
- table
- metal Slinky spring
- plastic Slinky spring
- tape

Instructions

1. With a friend, stretch out a metal Slinky spring over the table. Make it straight and reasonably rigid. Each of you should grab a few coils.

2. Demonstrate a P-wave. Hold one end of the spring and make sure it is perfectly still. Sharply tap the spring's open end with your free hand and watch the pattern of movement from your friend and back. One coil moves close to the next (compression), and then appears to move away (dilation) as the next coil transfers the com-

pression down the line. Notice that your P-wave travels in the same direction as the tap.

3. Demonstrate an S-wave. Hold the spring still, then quickly move one end back and forth once. Notice that S-waves don't travel in the line made by the spring. The wave travels along the spring, transferring a side-to-side wiggle as it moves. Notice also that S-waves take longer to travel the same distance as P-waves.

4. Wave speed and duration can change significantly through different kinds of materials, such as the earth's different layers. To see this, use tape to join two different (metal and plastic) springs together at one end. Repeat steps 2 and 3, and notice how the wave's movement changes as it travels the length of the double spring.

East Han
Seismograph

MEASURING EARTH'S VIBRATIONS

Seismologists detect earthquakes using **seismographs**. These sensitive machines record the earth's vibrations. Scientists calculate the amount of energy released by the earthquake by reading the output of a seismograph. When you hear about an earthquake in the news, the story always mentions the size, or **magnitude**, of the quake and the location of the epicenter. Neither of these two measurements would be possible without seismographs.

Scientists report magnitude (M) using the numbered Richter scale. Earthquakes of less than 3.5M go unnoticed by people. Earthquakes above 6.0M are felt as significant shaking, and can damage roads and buildings. One of the highest magnitude earthquakes ever recorded occurred in Chile in 1960. At 9.5M, shaking lasted for several minutes, causing buildings along the coast to sink into the sand.

Such large earthquakes are very rare. The most active plate boundaries experience frequent, small movements that are detected only using seismographs. You can make your own seismograph to measure vibrations around your home.

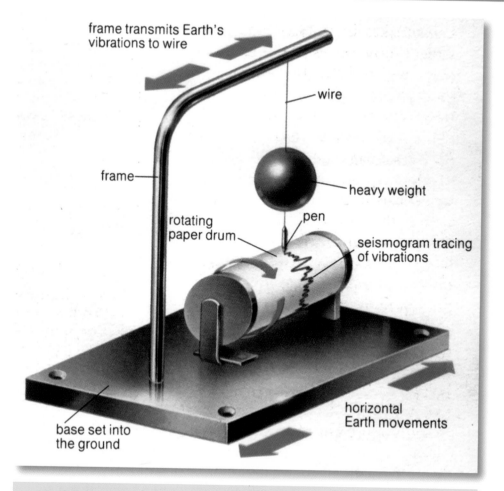

frame transmits Earth's vibrations to wire

wire

frame

rotating paper drum

pen

heavy weight

seismogram tracing of vibrations

horizontal Earth movements

base set into the ground

Materials
- cardboard box (shoe box size)
- scissors
- small plastic cup or Dixie cup
- pencil or pen
- tape
- string
- pebbles or marbles
- paper

Instructions
1. Cut the flaps off a cardboard box. Set the box on its side, open toward you. Poke two small holes on the side that is now on top.
2. Poke a hole in the bottom of a small cup, right in the middle. Poke two more holes near the rim opposite each other. Slide a pencil

through the bottom hole so that the writing tip sticks out below the cup. Secure the pencil with tape so that it doesn't move.

3. Thread the string through the two holes near the cup's rim. Thread each end of the string through one of the two holes at the top of the box. Now the cup hangs freely inside the box, supported by the string. Before you tie the string's ends, fill the cup about half-full of pebbles to weigh it down. Adjust the length of the string so that the tip of the pencil just barely touches the bottom of the box.

4. Time to record those earthquakes! Pick up the cup and place a piece of paper under the pencil to record vibrations. Leave the seismograph undisturbed for a while and see what happens. You may be surprised just how much vibration occurs in a still house! Experiment with your seismograph to see what it can detect. Place it on top of different appliances, like a refrigerator, a dishwasher, or a washing machine. You can also simulate an earthquake yourself by placing the seismograph on a chair and shaking the chair around.

MONITORING THE QUAKING EARTH

Because earthquakes occur near faults, scientists can keep track of where faults are—and where they are moving—by studying where earthquakes occur. The USGS monitors earthquakes around the world in partnership with other countries. By monitoring quakes, seismologists learn which communities are most at risk for earthquakes, and they can even predict where they will strike next. You can do this, too.

Materials
- world map
- markers or small labeling dots
- computer with Internet connection

Instructions
1. Go to the USGS web site to view information on earthquakes that have happened in the last 7 days (http://earthquake.usgs.gov/earthquakes/recenteqsww/Quakes/quakes_all.html).
2. Plot each earthquake on the world map. Use Google Maps (http://maps.google.com) to locate unfamiliar places.

3. Check the USGS site each day for one week and record new earthquakes on the world map.

4. The earthquake locations you marked are not randomly scattered over the earth's surface. Compare them with a map of the Earth's plate boundaries (see page 14).

5. During the last week, which areas in the world have experienced the most earthquakes?

6. Add more dots to your map, this time from another USGS site, the Volcano Hazards Program (http://volcanoes.usgs.gov/). You may want to use a different color. Volcanic eruptions are also the result of plate tectonics. In fact, volcano scientists rely on earthquakes to help them predict eruptions. Where have the most recent volcanic eruptions occurred? What do their locations have in common with the earthquake sites?

EARTHQUAKE EFFECTS: THE 2004 INDIAN OCEAN TSUNAMI

The tiny Burma Plate, under the Indian Ocean off the coast of Sumatra, had been wedged against the Indian Plate for hundreds of years. It finally gave way with a 9.3M shudder on December 26, 2004. When the crust moved up and down, it pushed up the ocean at that spot, creating a killer tidal wave called a **tsunami**. The wave spread out in a circle from the epicenter. Only 30 minutes after the quake, 65-foot- (20-meter-) tall waves crashed over the seaside town of Banda Aceh, Sumatra, killing tens of thousands of residents in less than 15 minutes. In all directions, the wave continued on at nearly 500 miles per hour (800 kilometers per hour). In less than a few hours, over

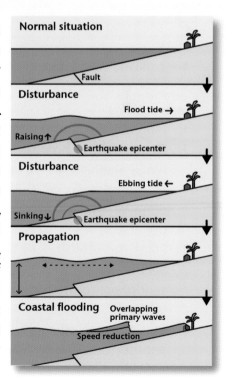

Normal situation

Fault

Disturbance

Flood tide →

Raising ↑   Earthquake epicenter

Disturbance

Ebbing tide ←

Sinking ↓   Earthquake epicenter

Propagation

Coastal flooding   Overlapping primary waves

Speed reduction

300,000 people were dead or missing, and the homes of more than 1 million people around the rim of the Indian Ocean were destroyed.

Tsunamis are not like surface tidal waves, which are created by the pull of the Moon's gravity. Tsunamis are born when earthquakes, landslides, or meteorites physically push deep water. They begin as small, fast-moving waves at sea. As they near the shore, the rising seafloor creates extra friction with the water, slowing down the bottom of the wave. This creates a sort of wave traffic jam. When the incoming high-speed waves slow down, they combine and grow taller, making killer waves up to 100 feet (30 meters) high.

To explore the destructive force of a tsunami, you can create a model in a wave tank. You will get wet performing this experiment, so consider filling the wave tank outside or use a bathtub.

Materials
- under-bed plastic storage bin at least 40 inches (1 meter) long (or use a bathtub, under **adult** supervision)
- 2 plywood or Styrofoam boards, 1 foot (30 centimeters) wide, cut to fit the width of the bin or tub
- duct tape
- modeling clay
- adhesive-backed sandpaper
- 2 plastic rulers

Instructions
1. Plug any holes in the bin with clay.
2. Fit one of the boards against one narrow end of the tank. Make a hinge against that wall (the "front" of the wave tank) about 3 inches (7 centimeters) off the tank floor by securely duct-taping a long edge of the board to the front bin wall. This will be the wave generator.
3. Place the other board at the back, at an angle with the tank floor. Secure it to the tank's wall and floor with duct tape. Affix the sandpaper to the surface of the board. This will be the beach, sloping upward from the seafloor.
4. Stand one plastic ruler up just beyond the wave generator, and another one just in front of the beach. Align the rulers' flat sides

parallel to the long tank walls. Secure the rulers to the tank's bottom with clay.

5. Fill the tank with water, 3 or 4 inches (7 to 10 centimeters) deep. Add small buildings or plastic toys to the beach to get a sense of a wave's destructive power.

6. Create a tsunami. Using your hands, gently push the free end of the board to the tank floor. Wait until all ripples have subsided, then rapidly pull the board up—like opening a trapdoor—toward the beach. Practice this move until you can make the biggest, most destructive waves. How tall are your tsunami waves at each of the rulers?

7. How does the sandpaper affect the wave shapes and strength? Remove it and create a wave to find out.

8. Experiment with different depths of water. How deep does the water need to be for your wave tank to create a tsunami?

EARTHQUAKE EFFECTS: A BETTER BUILDING

On December 7, 1988, a 6.8M earthquake rocked rural Armenia. The small town of Spitak was completely destroyed; the nearby city of Leninakan suffered heavy damage. More than 25,000 people died, and 512,000 were left homeless.

Less than a year later, a 6.9M earthquake—almost exactly the same energy—struck Loma Prieta, California, 60 miles (96 kilometers) from the millions of inhabitants of San Francisco. The Cypress Viaduct highway bridge collapsed. There were fires and damage to buildings, yet only 63 people perished.

Seismologists often say, "Earthquakes don't kill people. Buildings kill people." Earthquakes damage buildings, turning them into death traps. In Spitak, many deaths resulted because the cheap, brittle, old concrete in high-rise apartments snapped and crumbled under the shaking. In contrast, California laws require earthquake-safer materials in buildings. Steel-reinforced concrete and shock-absorbing pads helped high-rise buildings survive the Loma Prieta quake.

Can you design a quakeproof house? Try out different building materials and strategies.

Cypress Viaduct Highway Bridge, California

Materials
- craft sticks, drinking straws, chenille stems, Tinkertoy construction pieces, other building materials
- scissors
- clear tape
- table
- a friend
- stopwatch
- bricks
- newspaper
- sponge

Instructions

1. Build a single-story house out of whatever building materials you choose. Combine materials if you like (for example, try winding chenille stems around drinking straws). Start with four square walls. Secure the joints with tape.

2. Place the house on a tabletop, and shake the table hard. Have a friend monitor the quake with a stopwatch to see how long the house stands. Record the time, and note how hard you were shaking the table on a scale of 1 to 10.

3. If your house performed well, build a second story. If not, go back to the drawing board, using a different material or building technique.

Can you build a quake-proof structure?

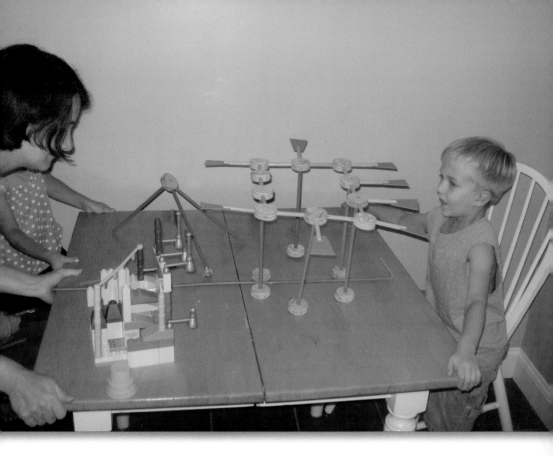

Cross-bracing (connecting opposite corners of the walls with extra material) can make a weak structure very strong. Repeat step 2.

4. Continue adding stories to your building until it no longer performs well on the shaking table.

5. Make several significantly different designs. Use different materials and build in different shapes (rectangular, triangular, cylindrical, or even unusual or irregular shapes). Which design lasts the longest?

6. In earthquake-prone areas, buildings are constructed with special ground supports. Try the following techniques and subject them to the shake table:

   a. Attach the house to bricks (representing a reinforced foundation) and place it on newspapers on the shaking table.

   b. Glue pieces of sponge to the bottom of the house (representing rubber and steel cushioning pads used in some buildings).

   c. Attach your house to the table with tape to represent deeply sunk foundations.

7. Using these steps as a starting point, make the most quake-resistant house you can.

EARTHQUAKE EFFECTS: LIQUEFACTION AND THE 1995 KOBE EARTHQUAKE

Japan is no stranger to earthquakes, and the country takes great measures to keep its people safe. Despite the country's efforts, on January 17, 1995, a 6.8M earthquake struck Kobe, Japan. More than 5,500 people lost their lives. Parts of the Hanshin Expressway toppled over. Roads, buildings, and equipment at the busy international port were destroyed, causing worldwide shipping delays. Repairs throughout the city cost over $200 billion.

Both the highway and the port were built on loose soil in ocean water. Normally, the soil could support heavy loads, but the 15 seconds of earthquake shaking was so intense that the soil particles separated from each other, like beans shaken in a jar. Water filled the gaps in a process called **liquefaction**, and suddenly the soil could flow like a liquid. Supports for roads and foundations for buildings collapsed in the soupy ground.

The best defense against liquefaction is to build on solid ground. When forced to build on sand or loose soil, engineers construct their own "solid ground" by building strong foundations or by sinking supports deep into the earth. You can demonstrate liquefaction—and how to overcome it—with a bucket-sized town.

The Kobe Earthquake twisted and tore the Hanshin Expressway like a concrete ribbon. The intense shaking liquefied the soggy, sandy soil, and it could no longer support the highway's weight.

Materials
- plastic bin or bucket
- sand
- board—plywood, Styrofoam, or cardboard (smaller than bin)
- scissors or saw and **an adult**
- blocks, plastic toys
- small shovel
- rice
- gravel
- garden soil
- clear plastic tube, about 6 inches (15 centimeters) long
- magnifying glass

Instructions

1. Fill the bin about ⅓ of the way with sand. Place the board on top of one side of the sand. Mark the outside of the bin to indicate where the board is.
2. Continue filling the bin with sand until it is about ⅔ full and the board is buried.
3. Saturate the sand with water. Let the goopy sand sit until it settles out and you can scoop all the extra water off the top. Smooth out the surface.
4. Build short towers and arrange plastic toys—animals, people, plants—on the surface. You can even use your earthquake-proof structures from the experiment on page 33.

5. Create an earthquake. Sharply tap the side of the bin repeatedly. What happens to the surfaces? Which buildings or objects would fare well in an earthquake on loose soils? How does the buried board affect them?

6. Use your bin and board to see whether other materials will undergo liquefaction. Test rice, gravel, and garden soil.

7. Use what you've learned about liquefaction to learn more about the soils in your area.
   a. Dig a hole in your backyard (or, with permission, your schoolyard) about 6 inches (15 centimeters) deep. Note as you dig if the ground is loose or well packed.
   b. Take about an inch of the soil from the bottom of the hole and carefully place it in a clear plastic tube. Move up an inch (3 centimeters) on the side of your pit, dig out a little soil there, and place it in the tube. Repeat until your tube is full. The soil in the tube should look like the side of your pit. Fill in the hole.
   c. Use a magnifying glass to look carefully at the soils in the tube. Do they look like sand? Clay? Or somewhere in between? Do you think your area would be in danger of liquefaction during an earthquake?

PREDICT THE NEXT "BIG ONE"

Nobody can say for certain when the next big quake will hit. Seismologists believe, however, that it can't hurt to guess, since the timing of earthquakes in certain areas seems to follow patterns. In 2010, Japanese scientists predicted that their next major quake would occur at Tokai, about 100 miles southwest of Tokyo. Tokai experienced some minor quakes in the 1970s, but it has not had a major one since 1854. Because historical records suggest that Tokai experiences quakes about once every 150 years, experts believe the time is coming soon.

In the United States, scientists target the small town of Parkfield, also known as the earthquake capital of California. Parkfield lies along the San Andreas Fault, about halfway between San Francisco and Los Angeles. In the last 150 years, Parkfield has experienced a number of earthquakes 6.0M or greater. Scientists study the history of Parkfield to predict when the next "big one" will occur there. You can do this, too.

Materials
- computer with Internet connection
- calculator
- notebook

Instructions

1. Visit the U.S. Geological Survey's Parkfield Earthquake Experiment site (http://earthquake.usgs. gov/research/parkfield/ index.php) for more information about the project. Note that Parkfield experienced strong earthquakes, of around magnitude 6, in 1857, 1881, 1901, 1922, 1934, 1966, and 2004.

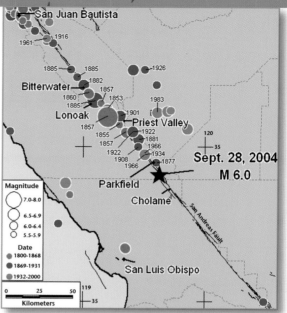

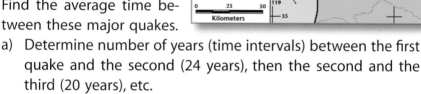

2. Find the average time between these major quakes.

   a) Determine number of years (time intervals) between the first quake and the second (24 years), then the second and the third (20 years), etc.

   b) Add all the time intervals together to get one big sum (24 years + 20 years + ... = ?).

   c) Divide the sum by the number of intervals (6) to get the average time between quakes.

3. To predict the next quake, add the average time between quakes to 2004, the year of the last quake. The answer will be the predicted year of the next quake.

4. With this method, you can predict the next "big one" for just about any earthquake-prone city. Use the USGS World Earthquake Information site (http://earthquake.usgs.gov/earthquakes/world/) to look up earthquake histories for one or more of the following seismic hot spots:

   a) Nicaragua

   b) Guerrero or Oaxaca, Mexico

   c) Yunnan or Sichuan, China

5. A program offered through the USGS web site allows you to make a map illustrating the probability of a strong earthquake for any ZIP code in the United States. Visit http://eqint.cr.usgs.gov/eqprob/2002/ index.php to use this tool. What can you learn about your area?

GET READY FOR AN EARTHQUAKE

By monitoring earthquakes that have already happened, you can see that some areas experience more earthquakes than others. The best way to survive an earthquake is to be prepared. Is your community ready for the next big one? Learn more about what to do in the event of an earthquake and pass it on!

1. Learn about the history of earthquakes in your area (http://earthquake.usgs.gov/earthquakes/states/). How often do they occur? What special problems might earthquakes cause where you live?

2. Study government recommended earthquake disaster materials, such as those at the Federal Emergency Management Agency's web site (http://www.fema.gov/hazard/earthquake/).

3. What should you do in the event of an earthquake? Think about different places you are during the day (home, school, etc). Make a plan for your family and hold earthquake drills. Make an emergency kit with supplies and keep it where you can access it during an earthquake. Hold earthquake drills with your family so that everyone knows what to do. Ask your teacher if your class can practice, too.

4. Is your community ready to handle an earthquake? Interview your neighbors and friends' parents to find out what they know. Compare their knowledge with yours.

Make a poster or flyer reporting what you've learned. Ask if you can hang it up in your school or in public buildings such as hospitals, shops, or city centers. Don't be shy! Your actions could save lives.

What to Do During an Earthquake

Stay as safe as possible during an earthquake. Be aware that some earthquakes are actually foreshocks and a larger earthquake might occur. Minimize your movements to a few steps to a nearby safe place. If you are indoors, stay there until the shaking has stopped and you are sure exiting is safe.

If indoors

- DROP to the ground; take COVER by getting under a sturdy table or other piece of furniture; and HOLD ON until the shaking stops. If there isn't a table or desk near you, cover your face and head with your arms and crouch in an inside corner of the building.
- Stay away from glass, windows, outside doors and walls, and anything that could fall, such as lighting fixtures or furniture.
- Stay in bed if you are there when the earthquake strikes. Hold on and protect your head with a pillow, unless you are under a heavy light fixture that could fall. In that case, move to the nearest safe place.
- Use a doorway for shelter only if it is in close proximity to you and if you know it is a strongly supported, load-bearing doorway.
- Stay inside until the shaking stops and it is safe to go outside. Research has shown that most injuries occur when people inside buildings attempt to move to a different location inside the building or try to leave.
- Be aware that the electricity may go out or the sprinkler systems or fire alarms may turn on.
- DO NOT use elevators.

If outdoors

- Move away from buildings, streetlights, and utility wires.
- Once in the open, stay there until the shaking stops. The greatest danger exists directly outside buildings, at exits and alongside exterior walls. Many of the 120 fatalities from the 1933 Long Beach earthquake occurred when people ran outside of buildings only to be killed by falling debris from collapsing walls. Most earthquake-related casualties result from collapsing walls, flying glass, and falling objects.

If in a moving vehicle

- Stop as quickly as safety permits and stay in the vehicle. Avoid stopping near or under buildings, trees, overpasses, or utility wires.
- Proceed cautiously once the earthquake has stopped. Avoid roads, bridges, or ramps that might have been damaged by the earthquake.

If trapped under debris

- Do not light a match.
- Do not move about or kick up dust.
- Cover your mouth with a handkerchief or clothing.
- Tap on a pipe or wall so that rescuers can locate you. Use a whistle if one is available. Shout only as a last resort. Shouting can cause you to inhale dangerous amounts of dust.

© http://www.fema.gov/hazard/earthquake/eq_during.shtm

Books

Edwards, John. *Plate Tectonics and Continental Drift*. North Mankato, MN: Smart Apple Media, 2006.

Fraidin, Judy, and Dennis Fraidin. *Witness to Disaster: Earthquakes*. Washington, D.C.: National Geographic Children's Books, 2008.

Levy, Matthys, and Mario Salvadori. *Earthquakes, Volcanoes, and Tsunamis: Projects and Principles for Beginning Geologists*. Chicago: Chicago Review Press, 2009.

Osborne, Mary Pope, and Natalie Pope Boyce. *Tsunamis and Other Natural Disasters*. New York: Random House Children's Books, 2007.

Rae, Alison. *Looking at Landscapes: Earthquakes and Volcanoes*. London: Evans Brothers Limited, 2005.

Van Rose, Susanna. *Volcanoes and Earthquakes*. New York: Dorling Kindersley, 2008.

Works Consulted

Bakun, W. H., and A. G. Lindh. "The Parkfield, California, Earthquake Prediction Experiment." *Science*, vol. 229, August 16, 1985, pp. 619–624.

Bolt, Bruce A. *Earthquakes*. New York: W. H. Freeman & Company, 1993.

Bonnet, Robert L., and G. Daniel Keen. *Earth Science: 49 Science Fair Projects*. Blue Ridge Summit, PA: TAB Books, 1990.

Bozkurt, Serkan. "Earthquake Machine." United States Geological Survey. http://quake.wr.usgs.gov/research/deformation/modeling/eqmodel. html

Braile, Lawrence W. "Seismic Waves and the Slinky: A Guide for Teachers." Purdue University, March 2006. http://web.ics.purdue.edu/~braile/ edumod/slinky/slinky4.doc

Dargush, Gary, Kathy Donnatin, Donna Lico, and Tori Zobel. "Building Structure Exercise." MCEER Information Service, 2009. http://mceer. buffalo.edu/infoservice/Education/structureLessonPlan.asp

The Earth. Edited by Peter J. Smith. New York: Macmillan Publishing Company, 1986.

Erickson, Jon. *Rock Formations and Unusual Geologic Structures*. New York: Checkmark Books, 2001.

Golden, Frederic. *The Trembling Earth: Probing and Predicting Quakes*. New York: Charles Scribner's Sons, 1983.

Hamilton, Rosanna. "Earth's Interior and Plate Tectonics." *Views of the Solar System*, http://www.solarviews.com/eng/earthint.htm

Kious, W. Jacqueline, and Robert I. Tilling. "This Dynamic Earth: The Story of Plate Tectonics." United States Geological Survey, January 13, 2009. http://pubs.usgs.gov/gip/dynamic/historical.html

Lamborne, Helen. "Tsunami: Anatomy of a Disaster." *BBC News*, March 27, 2005. http://news.bbc.co.uk/2/hi/science/nature/4381395.stm

Lynch, David K. "The San Andreas Fault." *Geology.com*, http://geology.com/articles/san-andreas-fault.shtml

McMenamin, Mark A.S. *Science 101: Geology*. New York: HarperCollins, 2007.

Plate Tectonics: An Insider's History of the Modern Theory of the Earth. Edited by Naomi Oreskes. Boulder, CO: Westview Press, 2001.

Sharp, Len, Robert Allers, Borys Browar, Daniel Parke, John Rice, and Richard Thomas. "Soil School Exercise." MCEER Information Service, http://mceer.buffalo.edu/infoservice/Education/soilLessonPlan.asp

"Tsunami! Sumatra 2004." University of Washington Earth and Space Sciences, http://www.ess.washington.edu/tsunami/Sumatra.htm

United States Geological Survey. "Latest Earthquakes in the World—Past 7 Days." http://earthquake.usgs.gov/earthquakes/recenteqsww/Quakes/quakes_all.html

Wood, Robert Muir. *Earthquakes and Volcanoes*. New York: Weidenfeld & Nicolson, 1987.

On the Internet

FEMA for Kids—Earthquake Legends
http://www.fema.gov/kids/eqlegnd.htm

Seismology Animations
http://www.iris.edu/hq/programs/education_and_outreach/animations

Smithsonian Institution—This Dynamic Planet
http://mineralsciences.si.edu/tdpmap/

United States Geological Survey—Earthquakes for Kids
http://earthquake.usgs.gov/learning/kids/

Wicker, Crystal. "Weather Wiz Kids." WRTV-6 Indianapolis
http://www.weatherwizkids.com/weather-earthquake.htm

asthenosphere (as-THEH-nuh-sfeer)—Region of the Earth's upper mantle just below the lithosphere, made of rock so hot that it can slowly flow.

continental collision (kon-tih-NEN-tul koh-LIH-zhun)—The pushing of two continental plates against each other.

convection (kon-VEK-shun)—Circular movement within a fluid, from a hot area to a cool area and back again.

divergent boundary (dy-VER-jent BOWND-ree)—The area between two plates that are moving away from each other.

elastic rebound (ee-LAS-tik REE-bownd)—Geologic theory that explains how energy builds up in tectonic plates and then suddenly releases it.

epicenter (EH-pih-sen-ter)—The point on the earth's surface above the focus of an earthquake.

fault—An area where Earth's crust is broken, such as between two tectonic plates.

focus (FOH-kus)—The point in the earth at which an earthquake occurs.

liquefaction (lih-kwih-FAK-shun)—The change in behavior of loose, water-soaked soils from that of a solid to that of a liquid.

lithosphere (LITH-oh-sfeer)—The uppermost layer of the earth containing the continental and oceanic plates.

magnitude (MAG-nih-tood)—A measure of the amount of energy released by an earthquake, as indicated on the Richter scale.

mantle (MAN-tul)—The thick, hot layer of partially molten rock under the lithosphere.

plate tectonics (tek-TAH-niks)—Geologic theory suggesting that the continents and oceans are on huge rafts of rock. These rafts, or plates, move very slowly on currents of magma in the asthenosphere.

seismograph (SYZ-moh-graf)—An instrument that detects and records vibrations and movements in the earth, especially during an earthquake.

seismologist (syz-MAH-luh-jist)—A scientist who studies earthquakes and their effects.

subduction (sub-DUK-shun) **zone**—The area where one tectonic plate is forced under another.

transform fault—The area where two plates slide against each other.

tsunami (soo-NAH-mee)—A large, often destructive, sea wave produced by a submarine earthquake, subsidence, or volcanic eruption.

ABOUT THE AUTHOR

As a kid, Claire O'Neal enjoyed collecting rocks and minerals with her brother. She grew up and married a geologist. Claire holds degrees in English and biology from Indiana University, and a Ph.D. in chemistry from the University of Washington. She has written over a dozen books for Mitchell Lane Publishers, including *Rocks and Minerals* and *Volcanoes* in this series, and *Genetics* and *Exploring Earth's Biomes* in Life Science Projects for Kids. She experienced the 6.8M Nisqually Earthquake in Washington on February 28, 2001, diving under a desk during her chemistry class. She now lives in tectonically boring Delaware with her husband and two young sons.